EASY INSTRUMENTAL DUETS

# CHART HITS FOR TWO

Arrangements by Peter Deneff

ISBN 978-1-70516-831-8

Visit Hal Leonard Online at
**www.halleonard.com**

World headquarters, contact:
**Hal Leonard**
7777 West Bluemound Road
Milwaukee, WI 53213
Email: info@halleonard.com

In Europe contact:
**Hal Leonard Europe Limited**
1 Red Place
London, W1K 6PL
Email: info@halleonardeurope.com

In Australia contact:
**Hal Leonard Australia Pty. Ltd.**
4 Lentara Court
Cheltenham, Victoria, 3192 Australia
Email: info@halleonard.com.au

# ALL TOO WELL

CLARINETS

Words and Music by TAYLOR SWIFT
and LIZ ROSE

3

# BAD HABITS

CLARINETS

Words and Music by ED SHEERAN,
JOHNNY McDAID and FRED GIBSON

# BANG!

CLARINETS

Words and Music by ADAM METZGER,
JACK METZGER and RYAN METZGER

# BELIEVER

CLARINETS

Words and Music by DAN REYNOLDS,
WAYNE SERMON, BEN McKEE,
DANIEL PLATZMAN, JUSTIN TRANTOR,
MATTIAS LARSSON and ROBIN FREDRICKSSON

# BLINDING LIGHTS

CLARINETS

Words and Music by ABEL TESFAYE,
MAX MARTIN, JASON QUENNEVILLE,
OSCAR HOLTER and AHMAD BALSHE

# DESPACITO

CLARINETS

Words and Music by LUIS FONSI,
ERIKA ENDER, JUSTIN BIEBER, JASON BOYD,
MARTY JAMES GARTON and RAMÓN AYALA

# DRIVERS LICENSE

CLARINETS

Words and Music by OLIVIA RODRIGO
and DANIEL NIGRO

# DYNAMITE

CLARINETS

Words and Music by JESSICA AGOMBAR<br>and DAVID STEWART

**Moderately fast**

# EASY ON ME

CLARINETS

Words and Music by ADELE ADKINS
and GREG KURSTIN

# HAPPIER THAN EVER

CLARINETS

Words and Music by BILLIE EILISH O'CONNELL
and FINNEAS O'CONNELL

# HAVANA

CLARINETS

Words and Music by CAMILA CABELLO, LOUIS BELL,
PHARRELL WILLIAMS, ADAM FEENEY, ALI TAMPOSI,
JEFFERY LAMAR WILLIAMS, BRIAN LEE, ANDREW WOTMAN,
BRITTANY HAZZARD and KAAN GUNESBERK

# HEAT WAVES

CLARINETS

Words and Music by
DAVE BAYLEY

# HIGH HOPES

CLARINETS

Words and Music by BRENDON URIE,
WILLIAM LOBBAN BEAN, JONAS JEBERG,
SAMUEL HOLLANDER, JACOB SINCLAIR,
JENNY OWEN YOUNGS, ILSEY JUBER,
LAUREN PRITCHARD and TAYLA PARX

D.S. al Fine

# LOOK WHAT YOU MADE ME DO

CLARINETS

Words and Music by TAYLOR SWIFT,
JACK ANTONOFF, RICHARD FAIRBRASS,
FRED FAIRBRASS and ROB MANZOLI

**Moderately fast**

# MILLION REASONS

CLARINETS

Words and Music by STEFANI GERMANOTTA,
MARK RONSON and HILLARY LINDSEY

**Moderately slow, in 2**

# NO TIME TO DIE

from NO TIME TO DIE

Clarinets

Words and Music by BILLIE EILISH O'CONNELL
and FINNEAS O'CONNELL

# PERFECT

CLARINETS

Words and Music by
ED SHEERAN

**Classic Ballad**

# PERMISSION TO DANCE

CLARINETS

Words and Music by ED SHEERAN,
JOHNNY McDAID, STEVE MAC
and JENNA ANDREWS

# SEÑORITA

CLARINETS

Words and Music by CAMILA CABELLO,
CHARLOTTE AITCHISON, JACK PATTERSON,
SHAWN MENDES, MAGNUS HØIBERG,
BENJAMIN LEVIN, ALI TAMPOSI
and ANDREW WOTMAN

**Moderate Latin groove**

# SHALLOW

from A STAR IS BORN

CLARINETS

Words and Music by STEFANI GERMANOTTA,
MARK RONSON, ANDREW WYATT
and ANTHONY ROSSOMANDO

# SURFACE PRESSURE
from ENCANTO

CLARINETS

Music and Lyrics by
LIN-MANUEL MIRANDA

# TOO GOOD AT GOODBYES

Clarinets

Words and Music by SAM SMITH,
TOR HERMANSEN, MIKKEL ERIKSEN
and JAMES NAPIER

**Pop Ballad**

# WE DON'T TALK ABOUT BRUNO

from ENCANTO

Music and Lyrics by
LIN-MANUEL MIRANDA

CLARINETS